Sells A Lot: Achieve Anything You Want"

Johnathan A. Barnes

TABLE OF CONTENTS

INTRODUCTION
The Art of Selling

Selling is a skill as old as civilization itself, yet it remains one of the most dynamic and applicable disciplines in the ultramodern world. From the bustling requests of ancient Rome to the digital stores of the 21st century, the art of selling has evolved, but its core principles remain confirmed in the wisdom and psychology of persuasion. In this 800- word disquisition, we claw into the complications of selling, its elaboration, and the dateless ways that make it a vital skill in any business or particular bid. Selling isn't just about swapping goods or services for plutocrat; it's a multifaceted discipline that intertwines economics, psychology, and communication. To exceed in this art, one must first understand the abecedarian principle the client is at the center of every sale. Whether dealing a product, service, or idea, the focus must always be on meeting the client's requirements and solicitations. The elaboration of Dealing Throughout history, selling has taken numerous forms. In ancient times, dealers bartered goods in original requests, counting on particular seductiveness and character to make trust. Fast forward to the artificial revolution, and we witnessed the rise of mass   product and advertising, changing the dynamics of selling. moment, the digital age has steered in-commerce, where algorithms dissect consumer geste and epitomize recommendations. Despite these advancements, the core of selling remains constant   structure trust, establishing fellowship, and understanding client requirements. The elaboration of selling is a testament to its rigidity, with successful salesmen learning to navigate changing geographies while upholding these dateless principles. Psychology of Persuasion At the heart of dealing lies the psychology of persuasion. Understanding the mortal psyche is essential to impact buying opinions. One of the most influential numbers in this field isDr. Robert Cialdini, who linked six principles of persuasion

1. Reciprocity People feel obliged to give back when they admit commodity. Offering value, similar as a free sample, can produce a sense of debt.

2. failure The fear of missing out drives people to take action. Limited- time offers and exclusive deals valve into this cerebral detector.

3. Authority People trust experts. Demonstrating moxie in a field can make guests more open to your recommendations.

4. thickness Once people commit to commodity, they strive to remain harmonious with their once opinions. Gaining small commitments can lead to larger bones .

5. Liking People are more likely to say yes to those they know and like. Building fellowship and chancing common ground can increase your likability.

6. Consensus People tend to follow the crowd. pressing how others have served from your product or service can sway decision- timber.   Applying these principles strategically can significantly enhance your selling prowess. still, authenticity is crucial. Using these tactics without genuine care for the client's well- being can lead to distrust and damage your character.   Effective Communication   Communication is the backbone of selling. Successful salesmen are complete at active listening, empathizing with guests, and acclimatizing their communication to address specific requirements. Effective communication involves asking open- concluded questions to uncover pain points, furnishing results, and addressing expostulations gracefully. also, liar is a important tool in the art of selling. Narratives produce emotional connections and make information memorable. By weaving a compelling story around your product or service, you can engage guests on a deeper position and separate yourself in a crowded business. Rigidity in the Digital Age The digital age has revolutionized selling, introducing new avenues and challenges.   Social   media   platforms,e-commerce websites, and online commerce have expanded the reach of businesses. still, the digital realm also demands rigidity and a strong online presence. In the age of information load, deals professionals must cut through the noise and give value. Content marketing, dispatch juggernauts, and social media engagement are vital tools for erecting brand mindfulness and nurturing leads. Data analytics and client relationship operation(CRM) systems offer perceptivity into client gest, enabling substantiated marketing strategies. likewise, the arrival of-commerce has given rise toe-tailers who exceed at understanding algorithms and   employing data to optimize their deals processes. These businesses use prophetic analytics to read client geste and force requirements, icing a flawless shopping experience. In an ever- evolving business geography, the art of selling remains a dynamic and necessary skill. Its elaboration from ancient commerce to the digital age underscores its enduring applicability.

CHAPTER 1
Understanding the Sales Process

In moment's competitive business geography, learning the deals process is consummate to success. Whether you are a seasoned deals professional or just starting in the field, a deep understanding of the deals process is essential for achieving your pretensions and driving profit for your association. This comprehensive companion aims to anatomize the deals process, furnishing you with a 1,000- word disquisition of its colorful stages, strategies, and stylish practices. preface to the Deals Process The deals process is a methodical approach that deals professionals follow to convert leads into paying guests. It isn't a one- size- fits- all model but rather a flexible frame that can be acclimated to different diligence, products, and client types. The core ideal of any deals process is to identify implicit guests, engage with them, understand their requirements, present a result, and eventually close the trade.

The Stages of the Deals Process

1. Prospecting : This is the original stage of the deals process, where salesmen identify implicit leads or prospects. It involves probing target requests, diligence, and individualities who might be interested in your product or service.

2. Qualification : In this stage, leads are estimated to determine if they meet specific criteria that make them more likely to come paying guests. This helps deals professionals prioritize their sweats and coffers.

3. Discovery : During the discovery phase, salesmen engage with good leads to understand their requirements, challenges, and pain points. This step is pivotal for acclimatizing the deals approach and proposing a applicable result.

4. Donation : Then, deals professionals present their product or service as a result to the prospect's problems. This involves showcasing the features, benefits, and value proposition of what you are offering.

5. Handling expostulations : It's common for prospects to have enterprises or expostulations at this stage. salesmen should be prepared to address these expostulations, furnishing consolation and information to palliate any dubieties.

6. Ending : The ending stage is where the factual trade takes place. Deals professionals use colorful ways to ask for the order or commitment from the prospect. This could be a inked contract, a purchase order, or any other form of agreement.

7. Follow- Up : After the trade is closed, it's essential to maintain a relationship with the client. This involves post-sale support, icing client satisfaction, and potentially upselling or cross-selling fresh products or services.

8. Referrals : Happy guests can come lawyers for your brand, generating referrals and new leads. Encouraging referrals is a critical part of the deals process that can lead to a nonstop cycle of growth.

The Psychology of Selling

Selling isn't just about products or services; it's about understanding mortal geste, provocations, and feelings. The psychology of selling delves deep into the complications of mortal nature to help salesmen connect with guests on a profound position. In this 1000- word disquisition, we will uncover the essential principles and strategies that bolster the psychology of selling.

1. Building Rapport   The foundation of successful selling lies in erecting fellowship with implicit guests. Establishing trust and a genuine connection is crucial. salesmen must be compassionate, hear laboriously, and show a sincere interest in the client's requirements and solicitations. reflecting body language and tone of voice can also help produce fellowship.

2. Understanding Needs   To vend effectively, one must understand the client's requirements. This involves asking probing questions to uncover pain points, solicitations, and provocations. By aligning the product or service with these requirements, salesmen can demonstrate value and applicability.

3. Emotional Persuasion   feelings play a significant part in decision- timber. Effective salesmen valve into the emotional side of their guests, painting a pictorial picture of how the product or service can ameliorate their lives. Positive feelings associated with the purchase, similar as happiness or relief, can be important motivators.

4. prostrating expostulations   Resistance is a natural part of the deals process. salesmen need to anticipate expostulations and be prepared to address them. This requires active listening,   compassionate responses, and   furnishing compelling   results. prostrating expostulations builds trust and confidence.

5. The failure Principle   People are more inclined to desire   commodity when it appears scarce or in high demand. Deals strategies that   produce a sense of urgency,   similar as limited- time offers or low stock warnings,   influence this cerebral principle to drive deals.

6. Social Proof   Humans are   innately   told   by the conduct and opinions of others. salesmen can use social   evidence by showcasing positive reviews, witnesses, or case studies to demonstrate the product's value and   trustability. This builds credibility and trust.

7. Authority and Expertise   Positioning oneself as an authority in the field can boost deals. guests are more likely to trust and buy from experts. salesmen should showcase their   knowledge   and   experience   to inseminate confidence.

8. Reciprocity   Reciprocity is a   important cerebral principle where people feel obliged to give back when they admit   commodity. salesmen can offer value outspoken,   similar as free   coffers or advice, creating a sense of debt that can lead to a trade in return.

9. Anchoring and Pricing   The way prices are presented can greatly   impact   copping opinions. Anchoring involves presenting a advanced- priced option first, making posterior options feel more reasonable. Careful pricing strategies can guide guests towards asked choices.

10. Fear of Missing Out(FOMO) Fear of missing out is a potent motivator. Deals tactics that punctuate what guests might lose if they do not make a purchase can spark a sense of urgency. Limited- time abatements or exclusive offers subsidize on FOMO.

11. ending ways The art of closing a trade is a critical skill. colorful ways, similar as the assumptive near, where the salesman assumes the client's readiness to buy, or the trial near, where they test the waters, can be employed. Timing and reading the client's cues are pivotal.

12. Post-Sale Relationship The psychology of dealing extends beyond the original sale. Maintaining a positive relationship with guests post-sale is essential for reprise business and referrals. Follow- ups, substantiated communication, and excellent client service each contribute to this. The psychology of selling is a multifaceted discipline that draws upon mortal geste, feelings, and decision- making processes. Successful salesmanship isn't about manipulation but rather understanding and aligning with the client's requirements and solicitations. Building fellowship, addressing expostulations, and using cerebral principles like failure, social evidence, and reciprocity are essential factors of effective selling. By learning these ways and maintaining post-sale connections, salesmen can unleash the secrets to successful salesmanship and produce lasting client connections.

CHAPTER 2
Sales Strategies

In the dynamic and competitive geography of business, deals strategies serve as the guiding compass for associations seeking to achieve their profit pretensions and sustain growth. An effective deals strategy isn't a one- size- fits- all result but rather a precisely drafted plan acclimatized to a company's unique immolations, target request, and competitive positioning. This essay explores the multifaceted world of deals strategies, probing into the crucial factors that make them successful, the significance of understanding your request, the part of technology in ultramodern deals, and the elaboration of ethical considerations in deals practices. Key factors of Successful Deals Strategies Successful deals strategies are erected upon several abecedarian factors that inclusively drive the association towards its objects.

These factors include ;

1. Clear objective : Deals strategies must begin with a clear understanding of the association's objects. Are the pretensions centered around profit growth, request share, client retention, or all of the below? objects give a sense of direction and purpose for the deals platoon.

2. Target Market Analysis : Understanding the target request Is consummate. Detailed request exploration helps identify client requirements, preferences, pain points, and buying actions. It enables the acclimatizing of deals approaches to reverberate with implicit guests.

3. Value Proposition : A compelling value proposition

communicates the unique benefits and advantages of a product or service. It answers the abecedarian question of why guests should choose your immolation over challengers.

4. Deals Team Training and Development : Equipping the deals platoon with the necessary chops, product knowledge, and deals ways is pivotal. nonstop training ensures that the platoon can acclimatize to changing request dynamics.

5. Pricing Strategy : Pricing plays a vital part in deals success. The strategy should balance profitability with request competitiveness, taking into account factors like cost, perceived value, and pricing models.

6. Deals Channels : Determining the most effective deals channels(e.g., direct deals, online, retail, hookups) is essential. This decision should align with the target request's preferences and actions.

7. Client Relationship Management(CRM) : enforcing a robust CRM system helps in managing client data, tracking relations, and enhancing client connections, which are vital for long- term success.   II. Understanding Your request   In the realm of deals strategies, understanding the request is akin to having a treasure chart.

A comprehensive understanding of the request involves

1. request Segmentation : Dividing the request into distinct parts grounded on demographics, psychographics, or behavioral factors allows for targeted marketing and deals sweats.

2. Competitive Analysis: Studying challengers provides perceptivity into their strengths, sins, and request positioning. This knowledge aids in secerning your immolation.

3. client Persona Development : Creating detailed client personas helps in imaging the ideal client, understanding their pain points, and acclimatizing deals dispatches consequently.

4. Market Trends : Staying attuned to request trends and arising technologies ensures that your deals strategy remains applicable and adaptable. III. The part of Technology in Modern Deals Technology has revolutionized deals strategies in recent times. Then is how

1. client Relationship Management(CRM) Software : CRM software centralizes client data, streamlines communication, and enables substantiated relations, fostering stronger connections.

2. Deals Analytics : Advanced analytics tools give real- time perceptivity into deals performance, helping in data- driven decision- timber and deals soothsaying.

3. Marketing robotization : Integrating marketing robotization with deals strategies allows for individualized lead nurturing, supereminent scoring, and automated follow- ups, enhancing effectiveness.

4. Artificial Intelligence(AI) : AI- driven chatbots and virtual sidekicks help in handling routine queries, freeing up the deals platoon to concentrate on high- value relations.

5. E-commerce Platforms : E-commerce platforms have extended the reach of businesses by enabling online deals and expanding client access. The elaboration of Ethical Considerations in Deals Practices

In an period of heightened mindfulness and translucency, ethical considerations in deals practices have gained elevation. crucial aspects include ;

1. Translucency: Ethical deals strategies prioritize transparent and honest communication with guests. Hiding information or using deceiving tactics can damage the brand's character.

2. client- Centric Approach : Putting the client's stylish interests at the van of deals sweats builds trust and fosters long- term relationship.

3. Data sequestration : Compliance with data sequestration regulations, similar as GDPR and CCPA, is vital. guests anticipate their particular data to be handled with care and respect. Sustainability Sustainable and environmentally conscious practices are decreasingly important to guests. Incorporating these values into deals strategies can enhance the brand's appeal. Deals strategies are the backbone of any successful business. They give the roadmap for achieving profit pretensions, expanding request presence, and erecting lasting client connections. A well- drafted deals strategy encompasses clear objects, request understanding, technology integration, and ethical considerations. As requests continue to evolve, deals strategies must acclimatize and introduce to remain effective and applicable in the ever- changing business geography. Success in deals isn't solely about closing deals but also about nurturing connections, fostering trust, and delivering value to guests, thereby icing sustainable growth and substance for the association.

Setting Sales Goals

In the fast- paced world of deals, success is frequently measured by one's capability to meet and exceed targets. Setting effective deals pretensions is a critical aspect of achieving this success. Whether you are a seasoned deals professional or just starting in the field, understanding the significance of setting deals pretensions and how to do it effectively is essential for reaching your targets and maximizing your eventuality. Deals pretensions serve as the guiding light for individualities and brigades, furnishing a clear sense of direction and purpose. They can be a driving force behind increased productivity, provocation, and eventually, success. This composition explores the significance of setting deals pretensions and provides a step- by- step companion to help you produce, track, and achieve your targets.

The Significance of Setting Deals pretensions

1. Direction and Focus : Deals pretensions act as a roadmap, guiding deals brigades towards their asked destination. They help individualities and brigades stay concentrated on their objects and avoid distractions. Without clear pretensions, salesmen may find themselves wandering erratically in their day- to- day conditioning.

2. Provocation : pretensions give a sense of purpose and provocation. salesmen are more likely to be engaged and committed when they've specific targets to work towards. Achieving these pretensions can boost morale and job satisfaction, leading to increased job performance.

3. dimension and Evaluation : pretensions produce a frame for measuring success. They allow salesmen and directors to assess performance objectively. This, in turn, helps in relating areas that need enhancement and areas where you exceed.

4. Responsibility : Setting clear deals pretensions fosters responsibility within the platoon. When everyone knows what's anticipated of them, it becomes easier to hold individualities responsible for their performance. This responsibility can drive individualities to work harder and tidily.

Steps to Setting Effective Deals pretensions

1. Define Your objects : Begin by easily defining what you want to achieve. Your pretensions should be specific, measurable, attainable, applicable, and time-bound(SMART). For illustration, rather of saying," I want to increase deals," you might say," I want to increase deals by 20 in the coming quarter."

2. Break Down the pretensions : Once you have your primary deals thing, break it down into lower, practicable way. These lower pretensions or mileposts will serve as checkpoints on your trip to achieving the larger thing. For illustration, if your main thing is to increase deals by 20 in a quarter, you can set yearly targets to track progress.

3. Consider literal Data : dissect once deals data to set realistic pretensions. Understanding once performance can help you set attainable targets and avoid setting pretensions that are too ambitious or too conservative.

4. Account for External Factors : Be aware of external factors that can impact deals, similar as profitable conditions, assiduity trends, and competition. Your pretensions should consider these factors to insure they remain attainable.

5. Engage Your platoon : Involve your deals platoon in the thing- setting process. Collaboratively setting pretensions can increase buy- in and provocation. Encourage platoon members to give input and suggestions to upgrade the pretensions.

6. Regularly Review and Acclimate : pretensions shouldn't be set in gravestone. Regularly review your progress and acclimate your pretensions as needed.However, consider setting further ambitious pretensions, If you are exceeding your targets.However, rethink your strategies and acclimate the pretensions consequently, If you are falling short.

7. Give Training and coffers : insure that your deals platoon has the necessary training and coffers to achieve their pretensions. Investing in their development and furnishing the tools they need can significantly impact their capability to meet targets.

8. Examiner and Celebrate Success : apply a system to track progress toward your pretensions. Regularly review deals performance, and when mileposts are achieved, celebrate them. Feting and satisfying success can boost morale and provocation.

9. Stay patient and flexible : Deals can be grueling , and lapses are ineluctable. It's essential to remain patient and flexible in the face of obstacles. Use lapses as learning openings and keep your focus on the ultimate thing.

10. Seek nonstop enhancement : After achieving your pretensions, do not rest on your laurels. Strive for nonstop enhancement. Set new pretensions that push your platoon to reach new heights and stay competitive in the   request. Setting deals   pretensions is a abecedarian practice for success in the deals assiduity. These   pretensions give direction, provocation, and responsibility, making them essential for individualities and brigades likewise. By following the way outlined in this companion and espousing a visionary, adaptable approach to thing setting, you can maximize your deals eventuality and pave the way for uninterrupted success in the dynamic world of deals.

Prospecting and Lead Generation

Prospecting and lead generation are the lifeblood of any successful business. In a world driven by data, technology, and evolving consumer actions,   learning the art of probing and lead generation is pivotal for sustained   growth and competitiveness. In   this comprehensive   disquisition, we will claw into the abecedarian generalities, strategies, and advantages of probing and lead generation, painting a pictorial picture of why these practices are necessary for ultramodern businesses.

Understanding Prospecting and Lead Generation
Before we dive into the pros and cons, let's establish a common understanding of what prospecting and lead generation number.

* **Prospecting** * is the process of relating and assessing implicit guests or guests for your business. It's like criticizing for gold in a swash – you sift through a large volume of implicit prospects to discover the precious nuggets that can potentially convert into guests. Prospecting can take colorful forms, including cold calling, dispatch outreach, social media engagement, and attending networking events.

* **Lead generation** * on the other hand, is the methodical approach to attracting and converting prospects into leads individualities or associations that have expressed interest in your product or service. Leads are implicit guests who have taken some action to indicate their interest, similar as filling out a contact form on your website or subscribing to your newsletter.

** **The Pros of Prospecting and Lead Generation** **

1. Business Growth and Sustainability : Maybe the most compelling reason to engage in prospecting and lead generation is the eventuality for business growth. Without a steady sluice of new prospects and leads, businesses can stagnate or decline. New guests are the lifeblood of growth, and effective supereminent generation is the machine that drives it.

2. Effectiveness and Targeting : ultramodern lead generation tools and strategies allow businesses to precisely target their ideal guests. This reduces destruction of coffers on apathetic parties and increases the chances of conversion. For case, digital advertising platforms enable businesses to display advertisements only to people who match specific demographics or interests.

3. Data- Driven Decision- Making : Prospect and lead data are inestimable for understanding client actions and preferences. With data analytics, businesses can OK - tune their marketing and deals strategies, making them more effective and effective. This leads to advanced conversion rates and increased ROI.

4. Improved client connections : When done right, supereminent generation can grease meaningful relations with implicit guests. This allows businesses to make trust and establish connections, which are vital for long- term success. individualized communication grounded on lead data can make guests feel valued and understood.

5. Competitive Advantage : In a competitive business, the capability to constantly attract and convert leads can set a business piecemeal from its rivals. Effective supereminent generation strategies can be a significant source of competitive advantage, helping a company thrive indeed in crowded diligence.

6. Diversification of profit Aqueducts : A different range of leads and prospects can help businesses diversify their profit aqueducts. By targeting different request parts, a business can reduce its reliance on a single client base, making it more flexible to profitable oscillations.

7. Scalability : Scalability is a critical factor for growing businesses. Prospecting and lead generation can be gauged up or down grounded on the business's requirements and coffers. This rigidity allows businesses to respond to changing request conditions effectively.

The Cons and Challenges

While the advantages of probing and lead generation are substantial, it's important to admit the challenges and implicit downsides

1. Resource ferocious : Effective lead generation frequently requires significant coffers, both in terms of time and plutocrat. Businesses may need to invest in technology, staff, and marketing sweats to see results.

2. Data sequestration enterprises : Gathering and using client data for supereminent generation must be done in compliance with data sequestration regulations like GDPR. Mishandling data can lead to legal impacts and damage a company's character.

3. Overwhelming Amounts of Data : The cornucopia of data can be inviting. Sorting through and assaying the vast quantities of information generated by supereminent generation sweats can be a complex and time- consuming task.

4. Competition : As further businesses fete the significance of supereminent generation, competition for the same pool of prospects can be fierce. Standing out in a crowded request requires invention and creativity.

5. Lead Quality Vs. Quantity : Generating a high volume of leads does not inescapably guarantee success. The focus should be on supereminent quality icing that leads have a genuine interest in your product and service.

CHAPTER 3
Sales Funnel Management

In the world of business, deals are the lifeblood that keeps associations thriving. To efficiently convert leads into paying guests, businesses employ a strategic frame known as a deals funnel. This conception, deeply embedded in marketing and deals, attendants prospects through a structured trip, from original mindfulness to final purchase. Effective deals funnel operation is pivotal for businesses seeking sustainable growth and profitability.

Understanding the Sales channel

A sales funnel is a visual representation of the client's trip, reflecting the stages they go through before making a purchase decision. generally, it's divided into several stages, each with a specific purpose

1. mindfulness : At the top of the funnel, the thing is to attract implicit guests' attention. This is achieved through colorful marketing sweats similar as content marketing, social media, and advertising.

 2. Interest : Once apprehensive, prospects need to be charmed by your immolation. Then, businesses give precious information or engage the followership with compelling content, aiming to spark interest.

3. Consideration : In this stage, implicit guests estimate their options. Companies must give detailed information, case studies, and comparisons to move prospects that their product or service is the stylish choice.

4. Intent : At this point, prospects show a clear intention to buy. They may request a   rally, a   quotation, or subscribe up for a free trial. This stage is pivotal, as it signifies a transition from interest to commitment.

5. Purchase : The moment of verity prospects come guests by making a purchase. This is the ultimate thing of the deals channel.

6. Post-Purchase : After the   trade, businesses concentrate on nurturing client connections. This stage involves   furnishing excellent client service, soliciting feedback, and upselling or cross-selling fresh products or services.

** The significance of Deals Funnel Management ** Deals channel operation is the methodical process of shadowing, optimizing, and refining each stage of the channel to maximize transformations and   profit. Its significance can be understood through several crucial points.

1. Effectiveness : Efficiently managing the deals channel ensures that   coffers are allocated where they're most demanded. This reduces destruction and maximizes ROI on marketing sweats.

2. Bettered transformations : By assaying and fine-tuning each stage, businesses can identify and address backups, performing in advanced conversion rates.

3. Client perceptivity : The deals channel provides precious   perceptivity into   client   geste   and preferences, abetting in the development of targeted marketing juggernauts.

4. Pungency : A well- managed deals channel allows businesses to prognosticate unborn profit with lesser delicacy, easing better fiscal planning.

5. Client Retention : Post-purchase stages of the channel help retain guests, promoting reprise purchases and brand fidelity.

Strategies for Effective Deals Funnel Management

To harness the eventuality of a deals channel, businesses should apply colorful strategies

1. Segmentation : Tailor marketing dispatches and content to different stages of the channel and specific client parts. This ensures applicability and resonates with the followership.

2. Lead Nurturing : Nurture leads through substantiated communication, similar as dispatch marketing and retargeting advertisements, to guide them through the channel.

3. A/ B Testing : Continuously test and optimize rudiments like captions, images, and calls- to- action to determine what resonates stylish with your followership.

4. Data Analytics : influence analytics tools to gain perceptivity into client geste and acclimate your deals channel consequently.

5. Deals and Marketing Alignment : Foster collaboration between deals and marketing brigades to insure a flawless transition of leads from one stage to another.

6. Robotization : Use marketing robotization software to streamline repetitious tasks, similar as supereminent scoring and dispatch juggernauts, freeing up time for further strategic conditioning.

7. Client Feedback : Solicit feedback from guests to understand pain points and areas for enhancement within the channel.

Challenges in Deals Funnel Management

While deals channel operation offers multitudinous benefits, it comes with its fair share of challenges

1. Complexity : Managing a deals channel can be complex, especially for businesses with multiple products or services and different client parts.

2. Constant adaption : The digital geography and client geste are ever- evolving. conforming the channel to these changes requires nonstop trouble.

3. Resource ferocious : Effective channel operation may bear significant coffers, including time, labor force, and technology.

4. Measuring ROI : It can be grueling to trait deals and transformations to specific marketing sweats directly. Deals channel operation is a dynamic and essential aspect of ultramodern business operations. It enables associations to guide prospects through a structured trip, eventually leading to increased transformations and profit. By understanding the stages of the channel, enforcing effective strategies, and using tools and technologies, businesses can unleash the full eventuality of their deals channel and achieve sustainable growth and profitability in moment's competitive request.

CHAPTER 4
Building a Sales Team

In the dynamic geography of business, the success of a company frequently hinges on its capability to induce profit. Central to this bid is the construction of a complete and motivated deals platoon. erecting a deals platoon isn't just about hiring individualities to make phone calls and close deals; it's a strategic process that demands careful planning, reclamation, training, and ongoing operation. In this essay, we will explore the critical rudiments involved in erecting a deals platoon that can drive profit growth and insure long- term success.

1. Define Your Deals Strategy : Before assembling a deals platoon, it's vital to establish a clear and comprehensive deals strategy. This strategy should outline your target request, pricing structure, deals channels, and profit pretensions. Having a well-defined strategy will guide your platoon's sweats and help them stay focused on the company's objects.

2. Identify the Right gift : Opting the right individualities for your deals platoon is maybe the most pivotal step in the process. Look for campaigners who not only retain the necessary chops and experience but also align with your company's values and culture. also, consider diversity in your platoon composition, as different perspectives can lead to further innovative results and a broader client reach.

3. Training and Development : Once you've hired your deals platoon members, invest in their training and development. salesmen should be well- clued in your product or service, understand your target followership, and be complete in deals ways. nonstop literacy and skill development are essential to keep your platoon competitive in a fleetly changing request.

4. Deals Tools and Technology : give your deals platoon with the tools and technology they need to succeed. client relationship operation (CRM) software, deals robotization tools, and analytics platforms can streamline processes, enhance productivity, and give precious perceptivity for decision- timber. insure that your platoon is complete in using these tools effectively.

5. Compensation and impulses : An effective compensation and incitement structure can be a important motivator for your deals platoon. Consider a blend of base payment, commissions, lagniappes, and other gratuities that align with your company's pretensions and assiduity norms. This should incentivize high performance and price top players.

6. Setting Clear Goals and Metrics : Establish clear, measurable pretensions and crucial performance pointers(KPIs) for your deals platoon. These criteria should be aligned with your deals strategy and overall business objects. Regularly track and review performance against these criteria , furnishing feedback and coaching as necessary.

7. Effective Deals Leadership : Strong leadership is essential for a successful deals platoon. Deals directors should be endured, knowledgeable, and able of guiding and motivating their platoon members. They should also foster a culture of collaboration and nonstop enhancement.

8. Regular Communication : Open and harmonious communication within the deals platoon and between the deals platoon and other departments is critical. salesmen should partake perceptivity and feedback with each other and with the marketing, product development, and client support brigades. This collaboration can lead to a more client- centric approach and better results.

9. Rigidity and Inflexibility : In moment's fleetly evolving business geography, rigidity is crucial. Your deals platoon should be suitable to pivot and acclimate their strategies and tactics in response to request changes or unanticipated challenges. Encourage a culture of learning from both successes and failures.

10. Nonstop Evaluation and enhancement : Regularly estimate your deals platoon's performance and the effectiveness of your deals strategy. Be set to make adaptations as demanded. What worked in the history may not work in the future, so staying nimble and open to change is pivotal for long- term success. erecting a successful deals platoon is a multifaceted process that involves careful planning, reclamation, training, and ongoing operation. It requires a commitment to nurturing gift, furnishing the right tools and impulses, and conforming to a changing business geography. By following these way and fostering a culture of nonstop enhancement, your company can make a deals platoon that not only meets but exceeds its profit pretensions, icing long- term success in moment's competitive business.

Hiring and Training Salespeople

Hiring and training salesmen is a critical task for any business looking to drive profit and grow its client base. The success of a deals platoon can have a significant impact on a company's nethermost line. To insure that you make the right opinions when hiring and training salesmen, there are several crucial factors to consider. First and foremost, it's essential to define what you are looking for in a salesman. Different diligence and businesses may bear different skill sets and rates in their deals platoon. Consider the nature of your products or services, your target request, and your deals strategy. Are you dealing high- value, complex results that bear a exemplary approach, or are you in a high- volume, transactional deals terrain? Understanding your specific requirements will help you identify the traits and qualifications that are most important for your salesmen. Once you've established your criteria, it's time to start the hiring process. Look for campaigners who not only meet your qualifications but also retain excellent communication chops, adaptability, and a strong work heritage. Deals can be a grueling field, and successful salesmen need to be suitable to handle rejection and adversity with grace. Conduct thorough interviews and consider using assessments or part- playing exercises to estimate a seeker's deals capacities. likewise, artistic fit is pivotal when hiring salesmen. Your deals platoon will be interacting with other departments and representing your company to implicit guests. insure that campaigners align with your company's values, vision, and culture. A cohesive platoon that shares common pretensions and values is more likely to work well together and deliver harmonious results. Once you've named the right campaigners, it's time to invest in their training and development. Effective deals training programs should cover a range of motifs, including product knowledge, deals ways, expostulation running, and client relationship operation. The training should be ongoing, as the deals geography is continually evolving, and your platoon needs to acclimatize to changing request conditions and client requirements. Incorporate real-world scripts and part- playing exercises into your training to give salesmen practical experience and help them make confidence. give them with tools and coffers, similar as deals scripts, deals collateral, and CRM systems, to streamline their work and enhance their productivity. Encourage them to seek feedback and continuously upgrade their chops. Mentorship can be a precious aspect of deals training. Brace new hires with educated salesmen who can offer guidance and support. This mentorship can help accelerate the literacy wind and foster a sense of fellowship within the platoon. also, tracking and measuring performance is essential in the world of deals. apply crucial performance pointers(KPIs) to assess individual and platoon progress. These may include criteria like conversion rates, deals proportions, and client satisfaction scores. Regularly review performance data and give formative feedback to help salesmen ameliorate. impulses and compensation plans also play a significant part in hiring and retaining top deals gift. insure that your compensation structure aligns with your deals pretensions and motivates your platoon to excel. Consider offering lagniappes, commissions, or other impulses tied to achieving specific targets. Incipiently, rigidity is pivotal in deals. Keep an open mind and be willing to acclimate your hiring and training strategies as demanded. The deals geography is dynamic, and what worked history may not work hereafter. Stay informed about assiduity trends and stylish practices to stay competitive. Hiring and training salesmen is a multifaceted process that requires careful consideration of your business's specific requirements and pretensions. By opting campaigners who align with your company culture, furnishing comprehensive training and mentorship, and continually measuring and conforming to performance criteria , you can make a high- performing deals platoon that drives success and growth for your association.

CHAPTER 5
Sales in the Digital Age

In the rapidly evolving landscape of business, sales have undergone a profound transformation in the digital age. Traditional sales methods that relied heavily on face-to-face interactions, cold calls, and printed catalogs have given way to a dynamic and tech-driven approach. This shift has not only changed how businesses sell their products and services but has also redefined the very nature of customer engagement and relationship-building.

Digitalization has opened up a world of possibilities for sales professionals. The internet has become an invaluable tool, allowing companies to reach a global audience with unprecedented ease. Online marketplaces, social media platforms, and e-commerce websites have become the new storefronts, enabling businesses to showcase their offerings 24/7, transcending geographical boundaries. This accessibility has fundamentally altered the way customers discover, evaluate, and purchase products and services.

One of the key advantages of digital sales is the ability to collect and analyze vast amounts of customer data. Through analytics tools and customer relationship management (CRM) systems, businesses can gain deep insights into customer preferences, behaviors, and buying patterns. This data-driven approach enables personalized marketing and sales strategies, allowing businesses to tailor their offerings to individual customer needs. Consequently, customers receive more relevant product recommendations and experiences, increasing the likelihood of conversion.

Automation is another game-changer in the digital sales landscape. Repetitive tasks such as data entry, lead qualification, and email follow-ups can be automated, freeing up sales professionals to focus on high-value activities like relationship-building and strategic planning. Artificial intelligence (AI) and machine learning algorithms can also analyze data to predict customer behavior and optimize pricing strategies, further enhancing sales efficiency.

The emergence of e-commerce has reshaped the concept of the sales funnel. In the digital age, customers can enter the funnel at various stages, from awareness to consideration to purchase, and even advocacy. This nonlinear customer journey requires businesses to provide consistent and engaging content across multiple digital touchpoints. Content marketing, including blog posts, videos, webinars, and social media, has become a powerful tool for attracting and nurturing leads throughout the buying process.

Social media platforms have become hubs for customer engagement and brand building. Businesses can interact with customers in real-time, address concerns, and gather feedback. Influencer marketing leverages the reach and credibility of social media personalities to endorse products, bridging the gap between traditional word-of-mouth recommendations and digital marketing.

While the digital age has introduced many opportunities, it has also brought new challenges. The abundance of information available online means that customers are more informed and discerning than ever before. Sales professionals must be well-versed in their products, industry trends, and customer needs to build trust and credibility. Additionally, the ease of online comparison shopping has intensified competition, requiring businesses to differentiate themselves through exceptional customer service and unique value propositions.

Security and privacy concerns also loom large in the digital sales landscape. High-profile data breaches and growing awareness of data privacy have led to increased scrutiny of how companies handle customer information. Building and maintaining trust is paramount, and businesses must invest in robust cybersecurity measures and transparent data practices.

Sales in the digital age represent a profound shift in how businesses connect with customers and drive revenue. Leveraging technology, data, and automation, companies can reach a global audience, personalize interactions, and streamline sales processes. However, success in this new frontier requires a deep understanding of customer behavior, a commitment to transparency and security, and a willingness to adapt to an ever-changing digital landscape. As technology continues to evolve, sales professionals who embrace the digital age will be best positioned to thrive in this exciting era of commerce.

Leveraging Social Media for Sales

In moment's digital age, social media has come more than just a platform for particular connections and entertainment. It has evolved into a important tool for businesses to drive deals, make brand mindfulness, and connect with their target followership. using social media for deals can be a game- changer for businesses of all sizes, but it requires a strategic approach and a deep understanding of the platforms. In this comprehensive companion, we will explore how to harness the full eventuality of social media to boost your deals.

1. Choose the Right Platforms : Not all social media platforms are created equal, and each has its unique followership and features. To effectively work social media for deals, it's pivotal to identify which platforms are most applicable to your target followership. Research where your implicit guests spend their time and concentrate your sweats on those platforms. For illustration, if you are targeting a youngish demographic, platforms like Instagram and TikTok may be more suitable, while LinkedIn might be better for B2B deals.

2. Produce Compelling Content : Content is king on social media. To capture your followership's attention and drive deals, you need to produce high- quality, engaging content. This includes eye- catching illustrations, instructional vids, and well- written captions. Use liar to connect with your followership on a particular position and show how your products or services can break their problems or fulfill their solicitations.

3. Make a Strong Brand Presence : thickness is crucial to erecting a strong brand presence on social media. Use a harmonious brand voice, colors, and messaging across all your biographies. Your social media biographies should reflect your brand's values and charge, making it easier for guests to identify and connect with your business. Do not forget to optimize your biographies with applicable keywords and links to your website or online store.

4. Engage with Your followership : Social media is a two- way road. It's not just about broadcasting your dispatches; it's also about engaging with your followership. Respond to commentary, answer questions, and laboriously share in exchanges related to your assiduity. Building connections with your followers can lead to brand fidelity and increased deals over time.

5. Use Social Advertising : Social media platforms offer important advertising tools that allow you to target specific demographics, interests, and actions. Invest in paid social media advertising to reach a wider and further targeted followership. Platforms like Facebook, Instagram, and LinkedIn give robust announcement targeting options that can help you reach implicit guests who are more likely to convert.

6. influence Influencer Marketing : Influencer marketing has gained immense fashionability on social media. Partnering with influencers who align with your brand can help you tap into their engaged and pious follower base. Influencers can genuinely promote your products or services, furnishing social evidence and driving deals. insure that your influencer hookups are genuine and align with your brand's values.

7. Apply E-commerce Features : numerous social media platforms have integrated e-commerce features that allow druggies to shop directly from your posts. use these features to make it easier for guests to buy your products without leaving the platform. Instagram Shopping, Facebook Shops, and Pinterest Buyable Legs are excellent exemplifications of tools that can streamline the purchasing process.

8. Examiner and dissect Performance : Data is inestimable in social media marketing. Regularly dissect the performance of your social media sweats using analytics tools handed by the platforms or third-party results. Track crucial criteria like engagement rates, click- through rates, conversion rates, and ROI. Use these perceptivity to upgrade your strategy and make data- driven opinions. **9. Offer Exclusive elevations :** Allure your social media followers with exclusive elevations and abatements. Limited- time offers, flash deals, and social media-exclusive deals can produce a sense of urgency and drive deals. Promote these offers effectively and use compelling illustrations and copy to snare attention.

10. Acclimatize and Evolve : Social media is constantly evolving, with new features and trends arising regularly. To stay applicable and effective, be willing to acclimatize and experiment with new strategies and formats. Stay streamlined with the rearmost social media trends and incorporate them into your deals approach when applicable.   using social media for deals isn't just about posting content; it's about creating a strategic and holistic approach that aligns with your business pretensions. By choosing the right platforms, creating engaging content, erecting a strong brand presence, and exercising advertising and influencer marketing, you can harness the full eventuality of social media to boost your deals.

CHAPTER 6
Providing Exceptional Customer Service

Exceptional Client service is the foundation of any successful business. It's not just about meeting client prospects; it's about exceeding them. In a competitive request, businesses that constantly give exceptional client service stand out and make pious client bases. To appear exceptional client service, several strategies can be employed, encompassing every aspect of the client experience.

1. Understanding the client : Exceptional client service begins with understanding your guests. It's not enough to know their demographics; you must understand their requirements, preferences, and pain points. Conducting thorough request exploration and gathering client feedback through checks and relations is essential. This sapience allows you to conform your services to meet and exceed client prospects.

2. Empowering workers : Commission is a pivotal aspect of delivering exceptional client service. workers who are given the autonomy to make opinions and break client problems without constant supervision can give further individualized and effective service. This commission instills a sense of power and responsibility among workers, motivating them to go the redundant afar for guests.

3. Comprehensive Training : Training is the foundation of exceptional client service. workers should admit comprehensive training not only in company programs and procedures but also in soft chops like communication, empathy, and problem- working. Regular training updates keep workers up- to- date with evolving client prospects and assiduity trends.

4. Clear Communication : Effective communication is crucial to icing exceptional client service. insure that guests can fluently reach your business through multiple channels, similar as phone, dispatch, converse, and social media. Respond instantly and with clarity to inquiries and enterprises. Transparent and honest communication builds trust with guests.

5. Personalization : guests appreciate a individualized experience. Collect and dissect data to customize relations and immolations. Address guests by their names, recommend products or services grounded on their former purchases, and flash back their preferences. Personalization shows that you value their business and understand their individual requirements.

6. Anticipating client Needs : Exceptional client service is not just about addressing current requirements but also anticipating unborn bones. Use data analysis to prognosticate client trends and proactively offer results. For illustration, ane-commerce platform can recommend reciprocal products to a client grounded on their browsing history and purchase geste.

7. thickness Across Channels : guests interact with businesses through colorful touchpoints, from websites to social media to physical stores. insure a harmonious brand image and position of service across all channels. thickness builds trust and ensures that guests admit a flawless experience, anyhow of how they engage with your business.

8. Quick Issue Resolution : Effective problem- solving is a hallmark of exceptional client service. Train your staff to resolve client issues instantly and effectively. apply a clear escalation process for more complex problems to insure they're addressed instantly and to the client's satisfaction.

9. Solicit Feedback and Act on It : Regularly seek feedback from guests about their gests . Act on their feedback to make advancements. This not only demonstrates that you value their opinions but also helps you identify areas where you can enhance your service.

10. nonstop enhancement :   Exceptional client service isn't a one- time achievement; it's an ongoing commitment. Continuously assess and ameliorate your client service processes. Stay streamlined on assiduity stylish practices and be willing to acclimatize to changing client prospects.

11. Measuring Success : To appear exceptional client service, establish crucial performance pointers(KPIs) to measure success. Metrics like Net protagonist Score(NPS), client Satisfaction(CSAT), and client trouble Score(CES) can help you track client sentiment and identify areas for enhancement. furnishing exceptional client service is a nonstop trip that requires commitment, fidelity, and a client- centric approach. When formed, it can lead to increased client fidelity, positive word- of- mouth, and sustainable business growth .

Handling Customer Complaints

Handling Client complaints effectively is pivotal for maintaining a positive character, retaining guests, and icing business growth. we will explore crucial way and strategies to address client complaints with professionalism and effectiveness.

1. Hear laboriously : The first step in handling client complaints is to laboriously hear to their enterprises. Give the client your full attention, ask clarifying questions, and show empathy for their situation.

2. Stay Calm and Professional : Maintain a calm and professional address, indeed if the client is angry or worried. Avoid getting protective or combative, as this can escalate the situation.

3. Empathize : Express empathy and understanding. Let the client know that you authentically watch about their issue and that you are committed to resolving it to their satisfaction.

4. Apologize : Anyhow of who's at fault, offer a sincere reason. This does not mean admitting guilt but admitting the client's dissatisfaction and vexation.

5. Gather Information : Collect all applicable information about the complaint. This includes the client's name, contact details, and a detailed description of the problem or issue.

6. Assess the Situation : Once you have the necessary information, estimate the complaint to determine its validity and the stylish course of action.

occasionally, a quick result is possible; other times, a more in- depth disquisition is demanded.

7. Offer results : Present implicit results to the client. Be flexible and open to their preferences, if possible. insure that the results align with your company's programs and guidelines.

8. Take Responsibility : If your company is at fault, take responsibility and assure the client that steps will be taken to help a rush. translucency and responsibility make trust.

9. Follow Up : After the complaint is resolved, follow up with the client to insure their satisfaction. This demonstrates your commitment to their happiness.

10. Document the Complaint : Maintain a record of the complaint, including the details, conduct taken, and the resolution. This can be precious for tracking trends and perfecting client service.

11. Train Your platoon : insure that your client service platoon is trained in handling complaints effectively. give them with the tools, knowledge, and chops to address colorful situations.

12. Learn and Ameliorate : Use client complaints as an occasion for enhancement. dissect trends and common issues to make necessary changes in your products, services, or processes.

13. Use Technology : Consider using client relationship operation(CRM) software to manage and track complaints. This can streamline the process and help in covering client relations.

14. Help Rush : Take visionary way to help analogous complaints in the future. This may involve revising programs, enhancing training, or refining products services.

15. Seek Feedback : Encourage guests to give feedback, not only when they've complaints but also when they've positive gests . This feedback circle can be inestimable for nonstop enhancement.

16. Maintain a Positive reports : In moment's digital age, a client's complaint can snappily reach a wide followership. Respond instantly and professionally on social media and review platforms to cover your character.

17. Legal Considerations : Be apprehensive of any legal scores or regulations related to client complaints, especially if your assiduity is largely regulated. Handling client complaints is an integral part of furnishing exceptional client service. By laboriously harkening, staying professional, empathizing, and offering results, you can turn unhappy guests into pious lawyers. Flash back to learn from each complaint, ameliorate your processes, and constantly strive for client satisfaction to insure long- term business success.

CONCLUSION

In conclusion "Sells a Lot" encapsulates the essence of success in various industries. Whether in the realm of business, art, or even personal pursuits, the ability to sell a lot is not just a metric of monetary gain but a testament to one's ability to connect with an audience, meet their needs, and leave a lasting impact.

The notion of selling goes far beyond mere transactions; it embodies the art of persuasion, the science of marketing, and the heart of entrepreneurship. Throughout this essay, we have explored the multifaceted nature of what it means to "sell a lot," delving into its implications, strategies, and consequences.

One of the fundamental aspects of selling a lot is the understanding that it is not solely about profit, but also about value creation. Successful businesses and individuals recognize that to sell a lot, they must offer products or services that genuinely benefit their customers. This value proposition forms the core of their success, fostering customer loyalty and word-of-mouth recommendations that amplify their sales.

In the world of commerce, selling a lot is not an end in itself, but rather a means to a greater end: sustainability and growth. Businesses that prioritize ethical practices, environmental responsibility, and social impact are increasingly seen as leaders in their industries. Selling a lot, in this context, entails aligning profit with purpose and making a positive contribution to society.

Furthermore, the art of selling a lot is intimately connected to adaptability and innovation. Markets evolve, customer preferences shift, and technology advances at an astonishing pace. Those who consistently sell a lot are the ones who can pivot, embrace change, and reinvent themselves as needed. They understand that complacency can lead to stagnation, and they are willing to disrupt the status quo to stay relevant.

In our exploration, we've also encountered the importance of effective communication. To sell a lot, one must possess not only a compelling product or idea but also the ability to convey its value convincingly. Persuasion, storytelling, and marketing are essential tools in the arsenal of those who aspire to sell a lot. Whether it's a persuasive advertising campaign or a charismatic pitch, effective communication can be the difference between success and obscurity.

The concept of selling a lot extends well beyond the boundaries of the business world. In the realm of art, creators aim to sell their vision to a wide audience. Musicians seek to sell a lot of albums, painters aspire to sell a lot of paintings, and writers endeavor to sell a lot of books. Here, the emphasis shifts from monetary gain to the desire to share one's creativity and connect with a broad audience.

On a personal level, the pursuit of selling a lot can take the form of influencing change, inspiring others, or leaving a legacy. Leaders who sell a vision for a better future, activists who sell the urgency of social causes, and mentors who sell knowledge and guidance all contribute to the greater good by convincing others to join their cause or adopt their beliefs.

In conclusion, "Sells a Lot" encapsulates a dynamic and pervasive concept that permeates various aspects of our lives. It symbolizes not only the achievement of financial success but also the art of creating value, the commitment to ethical principles, the embrace of innovation, and the power of effective communication. Whether in business, art, or personal endeavors, the ability to sell a lot reflects our capacity to connect with others, meet their needs, and shape our world.

To sell a lot is to be persuasive, empathetic, and adaptable. It is to recognize that success is not merely about accumulating wealth but about making a meaningful impact. As we navigate an ever-changing landscape, the notion of selling a lot will continue to evolve, yet its underlying principles will remain constant: the pursuit of value, the embrace of change, and the power of human connection.